VOLCANOES

DISASTERS

Merrilee Hooker

The Rourke Corporation, Inc.
Vero Beach, Florida 32964

Edited by Sandra A. Robinson

PHOTO CREDITS
© Bern Pedit: cover; © Lynn M. Stone: p. 7, 15; © Tom and Pat
Leeson: p. 12, 21; © Breck Kent: p. 13; © Lisa Petersen: p. 17;
courtesy U.S. Geological Survey: title page, 4, 8, 10, 18

Library of Congress Cataloging-in-Publication Data

Hooker, Merrilee, 1955-
    Volcanoes / by Merrilee Hooker.
    p. cm. — (Discovery library of disasters)
    Includes index.
    Summary: Discusses types of volcanoes, how they are formed,
and famous eruptions and disasters.
    ISBN 0-86593-244-1
    1. Volcanoes—Juvenile literature. [1. Volcanoes.] I. Title.
II. Series.
QE521.3.H66   1993
551.2'1—dc20
                                                    92-43121
                                                    CIP
                                                    AC

Printed in the USA

TABLE OF CONTENTS

VOLCANOES

A volcano is an opening, or vent, in the earth from which **lava,** gas, rock and **ash** burst during an **eruption.** A volcano is also the mountain of rock and lava that forms around the opening. The volcano mountain usually grows in a cone or dome shape, as each eruption adds lava and rock.

The gases, rocks, ash and flaming lava that explode from volcanoes are extremely dangerous. A volcano can create a major **disaster,** causing great damage and loss of life.

Paricutin volcano erupting over Michoacan, Mexico

TYPES OF VOLCANOES

Active volcanoes frequently erupt. About 500 volcanoes throughout the world are active, including several in Alaska and Hawaii.

Dormant volcanoes are resting. They will probably erupt again some day. Lassen Peak in California is a dormant volcano. It last erupted in 1916.

An **extinct** volcano will never be active again. The deep, remarkably blue water of Crater Lake, Oregon, fills the huge **crater** of an extinct volcano, Mount Mazama. A crater is a huge bowl in the earth or in the top of a volcanic mountain.

Lassen Peak, a dormant volcano in Lassen Volcanic National Park, California

HOW VOLCANOES ARE FORMED

We can't see the tremendous activity beneath the surface, or crust, of the earth, but we know it happens. An earthquake reminds us that forces within the earth can cause it to crack and tremble.

A volcano reminds us that heat and pressure within the earth are so great they can melt rock and send it, along with other materials, flaming upward into the sky.

Melted rock—lava—may stream down the sides of the volcano and build up around the volcano vent. The lava hardens eventually, like dripping wax from a candle.

A fountain of flaming lava in
Hawaii Volcanoes National Park

PARTS OF A VOLCANO

A volcano has three main parts: the volcanic form, the **chimney** and the **magma** reservoir.

The outer part of the volcano, often a cone-shaped mountain, is the volcanic form. The long tube inside the form is the chimney. One open end of the chimney is deep in the earth—several *miles* deep. The other end is the volcanic opening, where the eruption occurs.

Magma is melted rock underneath the earth's surface. It lies in a pool, or reservoir. Under pressure, it travels from the reservoir, through the chimney, and out the volcanic opening to the surface.

Steam rushes from the chimney vent of a volcano in southwest Alaska

Snow-capped Mount St. Helens in Washington rose peacefully above Spirit Lake ...

... until May 18, 1980, when the mountaintop exploded and turned the countryside around it into a disaster area

VOLCANO LANDS

The earth's crust is made up of great rock plates. These plates move from time to time and grind against each other. Along their edges, volcano and earthquake activity is greatest.

Most volcanoes, like those in North America's Cascade Mountains, are along the edge, or rim, of the Pacific Ocean.

Many volcanoes erupt unseen under the sea. Sometimes, however, a volcanic cone rises above the ocean's surface.

The Hawaiian Islands and Alaska's Aleutian Island chain are among the islands created by volcanoes.

An eagle watches over Alaska's misty, volcanic Aleutians

ERUPTIONS

Some volcanoes erupt in a loud, fiery explosion. Black smoke, red clouds of steam, and burning rivers of lava gush from the vent. Deadly gas and ash fill the air.

Not all eruptions are so explosive. Each eruption is different. All volcanoes release steam and gases, but not all produce lava.

Volcanic ash and some types of lava make good soil and fertilizer.

Fire and lava burst from a raging Hawaiian volcano

VOLCANIC DISASTERS

Volcanoes have caused frightful harm, killing thousands of people. Italy's Mount Vesuvius erupted in the year 79. It buried Pompeii and Herculaneum under ash and lava. Eighteen thousand people died.

Mount Tambora in Indonesia killed 12,000 people in 1815. The volcano forced an incredible cloud of ash into the sky. It blocked enough of the sun's rays to make 1816 "the year without a summer."

The eruption of Krakatoa killed 40,000 Indonesian people in 1883. In 1902, the poisonous gas and hot dust of Mount Pelée's eruption killed 30,000 on the Caribbean Island of Martinique.

Lava from Paricutin nearly buried the San Juan church in Michoacen, Mexico

MOUNT ST. HELENS

The Mount St. Helens eruption in May, 1980, was the worst volcanic disaster in U.S. history. Beautiful, snow-capped Mount St. Helens had sputtered and hissed for weeks. On May 18 the mountain peak exploded.

The blast blew away the upper 1,300 feet of Mount St. Helens. A storm of gas, rock and ash, followed by rivers of mud, destroyed trees, lakes and streams.

Over 200 square miles of forest was flattened by the volcano. More than 60 people died.

Mount St. Helens erupted in a blast that knocked trees down as if they were toothpicks

STUDYING VOLCANOES

The scientists who study volcanoes are **volcanologists.** They watch volcanoes and look for signs that they may erupt.

Volcanologists use **seismographs** to listen for rumbles in the earth and to detect movements in the earth's surface.

Being a volcanologist can be dangerous. They often work on the slopes of volcanoes. Scientist David Johnston, while studying Mount St. Helens from six miles away, was killed by the volcano's eruption on May 18, 1980.

Glossary

ash (ASH) — tiny particles of volcanic rock released during a volcano's eruption

chimney (CHIM nee) — the tube in a volcano through which melted rock travels upward and to the surface

crater (KRA ter) — a bowl-shaped hole in the earth or at a volcano's opening

disaster (diz AS ter) — an event that causes a great loss of property and/or lives

dormant (DOOR mehnt) — a volcano that is "resting" but could erupt again

eruption (eh RUP shun) — the powerful release of such materials as ash, dust, gas, steam and lava from an active volcano

extinct (ex TINKT) — no longer existing; no longer active (volcano)

lava (LAH vuh) — melted rock that pours out of a volcano and later hardens

magma (MAG muh) — melted rock within the earth

seismograph (SIZE ma graf) — an instrument used to record the direction, strength and duration of an earthquake

volcanologist (vuhl kan AHL uh jist) — a scientist who studies volcanoes

INDEX